754

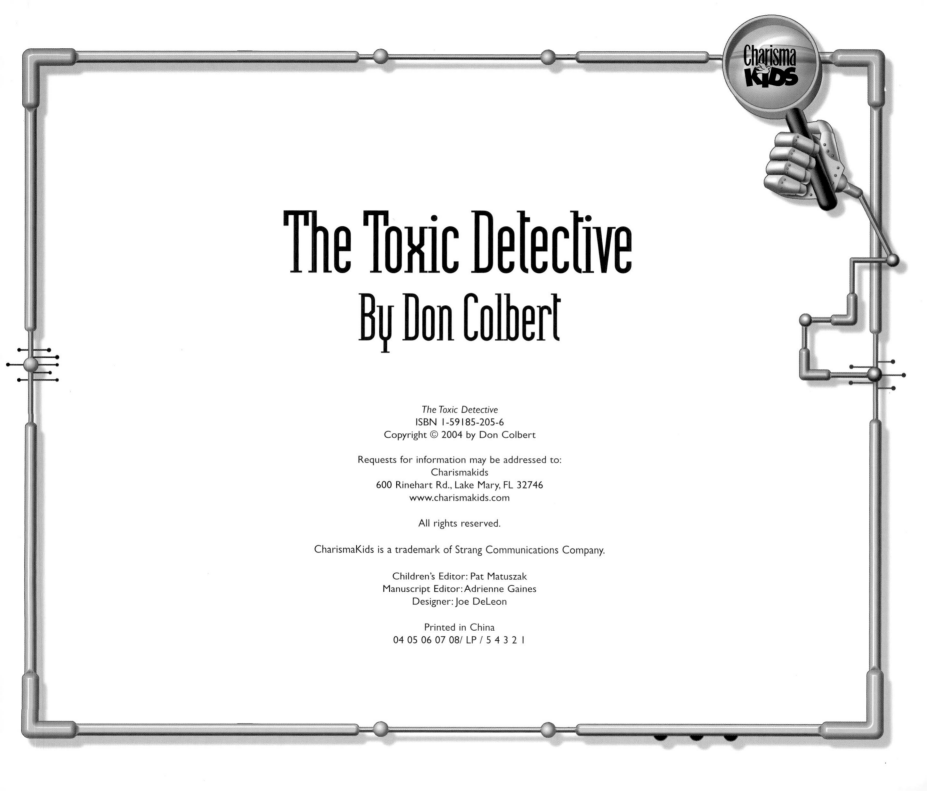

The Toxic Detective
By Don Colbert

The Toxic Detective
ISBN 1-59185-205-6
Copyright © 2004 by Don Colbert

Requests for information may be addressed to:
Charismakids
600 Rinehart Rd., Lake Mary, FL 32746
www.charismakids.com

CharismaKids is a trademark of Strang Communications Company.

Children's Editor: Pat Matuszak
Manuscript Editor: Adrienne Gaines
Designer: Joe DeLeon

Printed in China
04 05 06 07 08/ LP / 5 4 3 2 1

Miss Mulpit came into her cheery classroom ready to begin Sunday school.

"Good morning, class!" she sang out in her usual happy voice.

But the room was very quiet. No one answered her. She looked around.

"Where are the children?" she wondered.

She dropped her big lumpy craft bag on the floor.
It went clunk-crinkle-rattle-jingle.
She looked around the room again.
She peeped her head out the door.
But no children were coming down the hallway to her room.

"Hellooo…" Miss Mulpit called.

The empty hallway echoed hello back faintly.

"Well, how could everyone be late?" Miss Mulpit puzzled. She went back into the room and began to shuffle through her bag, looking for her cell phone.

Then Miss Mulpit's keen hearing caught a faint noise. It was coming from under the chair at the back of the class. She cautiously went back to see what it was.

She recognized the tennis shoes sticking out from under the chair.
"What's happened to you, Caleb?" Miss Mulpit asked as she
helped him sit up.

The boy could hardly speak. "I was coming to Sunday school when a big creature whooshed by me. It felt like the thing stole all my strength.
I could barely make it to the room and now I just want to sleep. Mmmm."
Caleb toppled back weakly to the floor with one eye opened and one eye closed.

Miss Mulpit quickly dialed her friend Dr. Colbert. She knew he could give her good advice.

Dr. Colbert hurried over to the Sunday school room from adult church, carrying his big doctor's bag. He examined Caleb carefully.

"Look at this: tiny specks of powdered sugar on Caleb's collar and raspberry jelly on the corner of his mouth. It looks like the Candy-Coated Creepie has been here. He tempts kids to eat things like pies, cakes and jelly doughnuts instead of fruits and vegetables. This makes them so weak that he can easily steal all their strength.

"The Creepie hangs out with a really bad crowd. If he's around, the Toxic Phat Daddy and the Drydrator won't be far behind. But never fear, my dear Miss Mulpit, I know someone who can help us find the rest of the kids. We'll call in the Toxic Detective!"

Dr. Colbert used his secret communicator to call Detective Doodad, who was known everywhere as the Toxic Detective. He could track down toxic health enemies with his amazing inventions.

A large eyeball appeared on the screen. "Doodad? Dr. Colbert here. There's an emergency at the church! We need expert toxin tracking help. Can you bring your toxin detecting gear and come right away?"

The eyeball moved back from the screen and a blurry face started to form as it answered,

"I'm on my..."

"...way!"

Suddenly a figure in a dark blue suit burst through the door of Miss Mulpit's classroom.

"Got here as fast as I could, Dr. C," the Toxic Detective said. "When I heard the Candy-Coated Creepie was in town, I knew we couldn't waste any time. **Do we have any clues?"**

"Miss Mulpit found Caleb here lying on the floor, exhausted," Dr. Colbert said. "I noticed he'd eaten a jelly doughnut instead of a healthy breakfast."

Detective Doodad peered at Caleb long and hard through his Toxi-oculars.

"I see what you mean, Dr. C. The Creepie has definitely been here. I suspect the Toxic Phat Daddie is around, too. See this grease spot on his shirt collar?"

"Caleb, where were you yesterday?"
the Toxic Detective asked.

"I went to Allie Gaines' birthday party,"
Caleb said. "Some of the other kids from
church were there, too. We had cake, hot
dogs and chips."

"Aha! This is beginning to make perfect
sense. I'm heading to Allie's house,"
Toxic Detective said. "There are
probably some more clues there.
I'll call you if I find anything."

In a flash the Toxic Detective arrived at Allie Gaines' house. He knocked on the door and Mrs. Gaines answered. "Hi, Mrs. Gaines," he said. "How are you this fine Sunday morning?"

"Not so good, Detective," she replied. "Allie woke up with a tummy ache today."

"Several kids are missing from Sunday school this morning," Detective Doodad told her, "and I'm tracking down the culprits responsible for their disappearance."

"You can look around. Nicole Green and Kennedy Carter were here yesterday, too." The detective stepped into the Gaines' backyard, and pulled out his Sniffometer. He peered around slowly, carefully looking for clues. Suddenly Sniffometer began to beep loudly. It had found something!

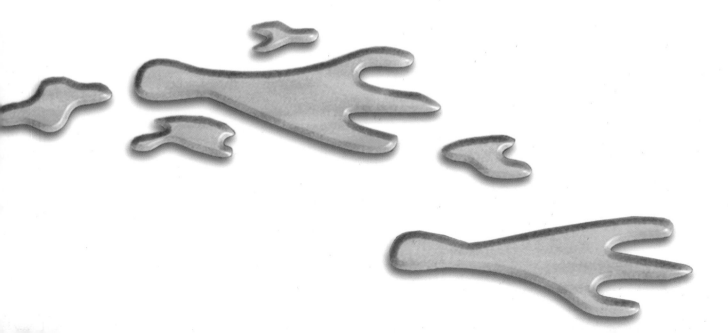

The Toxic Detective looked through his Toxi-oculars. There were drops of blue liquid in the grass and glowing footprints going away from the yard.
Mrs. Gaines called out, "Nicole's mom says she's home sick today, too."

"Aha," said the detective. "I've found toxic clues here, Mrs. Gaines. There was a lot of white sugar in the cake icing and chemicals and fat in the hot dogs and chips yesterday. That may be the cause of their tummy aches."

"That guy who sold me the party supplies did seem kind of strange," she replied. "He sold them to me for a bargain price, but a tummy ache is no bargain!"

Doodad nodded, "I suspect you were tricked by the Toxic Phat Daddie. He pushes fried foods high in fat and chemicals. They look tasty, but are not good quality protein, like lean chicken and fish."

The detective tipped his hat. Then he was off to Nicole Green's house in a whirl.

As the Toxic Detective stepped to the door, he could hear the television running in the background. He rang the doorbell, and Nicole's mom answered.

"Hi, Ms. Green," the detective said. "I've been on the trail of kids missing from Sunday school. Mrs. Gaines said Nicole was at home sick. Do you mind if I come in?" he asked. "I found something at the Gaines' house, and I want to see if there are more clues here."

"Sure," Ms. Green said, opening the door wider. Toxic Detective stepped inside. In the living room Nicole was watching television.

Sitting next to her on the coffee table was a box of Blue Ice drink.

"Just as I thought!" the Toxic Detective said. He called Dr. Colbert. "Dr. C, I found Nicole and Allie, and I think the Drydrator may also be on the loose. I detected drops of blue liquid in Allie's backyard, and now I've discovered a box of Blue Ice drink at Nicole's. The Drydrator tries to get kids to choose flavored drinks instead of pure water. They don't feel like playing outside or paying attention in school when their bodies get dehydrated and full of chemicals."

"You're right, Doodad," Dr. Colbert said. "Nicole needs to drink lots of water. That's the only way to fight the Drydrator."

The Toxic Detective turned toward Nicole, who was still staring at the television.

"Nicole?" he called.

But she acted as if she didn't hear him.

"Nicole?" he tried again.

Still no answer.

It was as if Nicole was hypnotized by the TV set.

Detective Doodad used his Spyzer-counter to pick up brain signals. It gave off steady beeps as he scanned near the TV.

Behind the set, a slithery snake-like creature coiled up like a cobra ready to spring. "I've never seen anything like this before," Toxic Detective said. Carefully, he picked up the snake with special forked-tongue tongs from his bag. He put it in a box.

As soon as he moved the snake, Nicole seemed to come out of her trance. "Detective Doodad! What are you doing here?" she asked.

"I've been looking for you and the other children from Miss Mulpit's Sunday school," he answered. "How long have you been glued to the TV?"

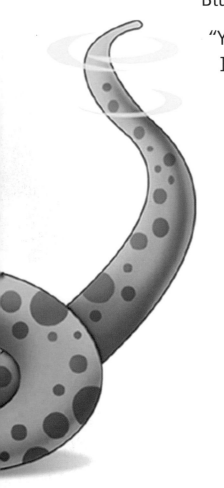

"I don't know. I woke up feeling so tired all I could do was sleep. My mom brought me something to eat and told me to rest. Then I drank some juice..."

"Blue Ice drink?" Toxic Detective asked.

"Yes, that's my favorite. I still felt tired and we were late for church. I watched TV. The next thing I knew, you were standing there with that box."

"Hmmm." Toxic Detective said. "I think I'd better call Dr. Colbert for this one."

He called Dr. Colbert and told him Nicole's story, including the part about the snake.

"Congratulations, Doodad. You've bagged Mezmer-Eyes, the TV trapper.
He sits behind the television and mesmerizes kids.
Mezmer-Eyes is one of the worst health hazard monsters because kids need exercise to grow healthy. Their minds also grow when they play together and use their imaginations to make up their own fun. If they spend all their time staring at TV, they can get overweight and lose muscle tone. That puts them at risk for a ton of diseases.
Bring that slimy creature here now, so we can keep him under lock and key!"

When Detective Doodad told Nicole's mom what Dr. Colbert said, she and Nicole agreed to limit TV time each day. Ms. Green said she'd make sure to give Nicole water and natural juices instead of fake flavor drinks.

"I have to go," the Detective said. "I hope I'll see you both at church next week."

The daring detective headed back to the church with Mezmer-Eyes in the bag.

But as he walked past the park, he noticed a little boy sitting on the swing set at the playground. He was all alone and looking sad. The Toxic Detective walked over to him and said, "Hi, there. What's your name?"

"Kyle," the boy sighed.

"I'm Detective Doodad. You look unhappy.   What's the matter?"

"Oh, it's nothing, I guess," Kyle answered.

"You don't look as if there's nothing wrong," Doodad replied.

"Well, there's so much happening. I have an all-star game Tuesday, and a science project due. My grades in reading aren't good. My little brother is always bugging me to play. I just can't do it all.

How can I be a good ball player, a good student and a good big brother all at the same time?"

"Do you know who Jesus is?" the detective asked.

"Yes," Kyle replied. "I believe Jesus died on the cross for my sins. I asked Him to come and live in my heart and help me to obey Him."

"Well, then, you've solved the most important mystery of all! You know you can pray to God. But did you know that you can give all your cares to Him? In the Bible, Jesus said, 'Come to Me, all who are tired and burdened down, and I will give you rest.'"

"How do I give my cares to Jesus?" Kyle asked.

"You can talk to Him through prayer. Tell Him all your worries and ask Him for His peace to be in your mind instead. Do you want me to pray with you?"

"Yes," Kyle nodded.

Detective Doodad prayed, "Lord Jesus, please take away Kyle's worries and give him faith that You will help him in all he's facing. Fill his heart with peace. Let him know how deeply he is loved by the One who made the whole universe. In Jesus' name. Amen."

"Wow, I do feel better! I thought of each problem. I pictured Jesus taking it off my shoulders. I'm going to talk to Jesus every day, so I can always feel this good. Thanks, Detective," said Kyle.

He jumped off the swing and ran toward home.

The next Sunday, Miss Mulpit walked into her classroom as cheery as ever. "Good morning, class!" she sang out in her usual happy voice. This time, the room was filled with children.

"Good morning, Miss Mulpit!" they replied.

Caleb was sitting up straight in his chair, paying close attention. Allie was there too, along with Nicole. Kyle, who was visiting the church with Detective Doodad, had a big smile on his face.

"It's great to see you all," Miss Mulpit said. "We're going to have a great class."

Health Chart

Snacks

Choose

Fresh fruit like apples, oranges, bananas and grapes.

Avoid

Candy, fried chips and donuts.

Cereals

Choose

High fiber cereals, whole grain cereals and old-fashioned oatmeal.

Avoid

High sugar cereals with marshmallows, artificial colors and flavors, sugar frosting and refined flour instead of whole grain.

Drinks

Children need 8 cups of water every day. If your water does not test within safe parameters, choose bottled or filtered water.

Choose

Natural 100% fruit juices, with no artificial colors or sugar added These also make great snacks when frozen.

Avoid

Carbonated drinks and drinks with caffeine.

Protein

Choose

Lean meat that is not fried, such as broiled and baked fish, chicken, and turkey.

Avoid

Fried meat and "mystery" meat mixes that are high in fat content and chemicals.